HOW TO TALK WITH ANYBODY

MASTER SMALL TALK, BUSINESS, SALES &
IMPROVE YOUR SOCIAL SKILLS AND MAKE
REAL FRIENDS

Jordan B. White

Table of Contents

TABLE OF CONTENTS 2

INTRODUCTION 5

CHAPTER 1. SPEAKING SKILLS 9
- KNOCK YOUR FEAR DOWN 10
- SPEAK UP! 12

CHAPTER 2. WHY ARE OUTSTANDING CONVERSATION SKILLS WILL CHANGE YOUR LIFE? 17
- THE MYTH OF THE SOCIALLY AWKWARD GENIUS 20
- CAN CONVERSATION AND SOCIAL SKILLS BE TAUGHT? 21
- TIPS ON HOW TO COMMUNICATE EFFECTIVELY 23

CHAPTER 3. COMMUNICATION SKILLS 29
- IMPROVE COMMUNICATION SKILLS 29
- GREAT CAREER 30

CHAPTER 4. CAREER SUCCESS 32

CHAPTER 5. START A CONVERSATION WITH ANYONE 36
- RAPPORT ACROSS THE ROOM 37
- MINDSET MATTERS 37
- COMMON GROUND 38
- A COMMON TOPIC HELPS 39
- CONCENTRATE ON SOMETHING PLEASANT 40
- ASK FOR ASSISTANCE 41
- DEVELOP CONFIDENCE 41

CHAPTER 6. DIFFERENT PEOPLE, DIFFERENT APPROACH 44

PERSONALITY TYPES 44

IDENTIFYING A PERSONALITY 45

CHAPTER 7. HOW TO AVOID BEING RUDE WHEN TALKING WITH SOMEONE   52

SPEAKING WITH POLITENESS... 52

BEING MINDFUL OF THE OTHER PERSON 55

UTILIZING PROPER BODY LANGUAGE... 59

CHAPTER 8. HOW TO BUILD CONFIDENCE 62

TAKE CARE OF YOUR BODY 63

WATCH WHAT YOUR BODY IS SAYING 63

START REPEATING SOME POSITIVE AFFIRMATIONS.................... 65

DRESS CONFIDENTLY 66

CHAPTER 9. PUBLIC SPEAKING 69

PUBLIC SPEAKING IMPORTANCE.. 69

ASK ATTENTION OF THE AUDIENCE BEFORE SPEAKING 71

IMPORTANCE OF BODY LANGUAGE IN PUBLIC SPEAKING........... 72

ASK QUESTIONS IN PUBLIC SPEAKING.. 74

CHAPTER 10. CHARACTERISTICS OF A GOOD PUBLIC SPEAKER...76

CHAPTER 11. GETTING AUDIENCES' ATTENTION 80

CHAPTER 12. MANAGE CONVERSATION WITH EVERYONE 88

DIFFERENT WAYS TO START A CONVERSATION 89

EFFECTIVE DISCUSSION 94

How to Improve Communication Skills of Individual or Organization? 97

CHAPTER 13. WAYS TO CONNECT WITH A LARGE AUDIENCE ... 101

CONCLUSION **105**

Introduction

The ability to actually communicate efficiently is perhaps the most important of all fundamental abilities. It enables us to pass information to others and to understand what is shared with us. You just need to watch a child listening eagerly to its mom and attempting to rehash the sounds that she makes to comprehend how major the desire to impart is.

At its most basic, communication is the representation of moving information from one location to another. It could be vocally, composed, outwardly, or non-verbally. Practically speaking, it is, in many cases, a mix of a few of these.

Effective communication may take a long time to master — if at all — anyone can claim to have mastered them at any time.

There are, in any case, numerous things that you can do decently effectively to further develop your communication abilities and guarantee that you can communicate and get information effectively. It's never a bad time to chip away at your communication abilities, and thusly, you might well find that you work on your personal satisfaction.

These abilities are required in practically all parts of life. Professionally, if you are applying for positions or seeking advancement with your boss, you will most likely need to demonstrate excellent communication skills. These abilities are required to talk appropriately with a wide range of people while staying in touch; demonstrate various jargon and design your language for your audience; listen effectively; present your thoughts appropriately; compose clearly and succinctly; and function admirably in a gathering. Large numbers of these are fundamental abilities that most businesses look for.

Great communication skills can work on your own connections by assisting you with grasping others and being perceived as an individual. Individual connections require correspondence, which is almost a given. The inability to talk has been blamed for the breakdown of quite a few organizations and relationships, but the capacity to listen is likewise a significant component.

Communication is also imperative in more extensive family connections, whether you need to talk about plans for occasions or guarantee that your teen kids are well and cheerful. These skills can guarantee that you can oversee connections with organizations and associations.

Throughout the span of your lifetime, you are probably going to need to cooperate with many associations and foundations, including shops, organizations, government workplaces, and schools. Great communication skills can facilitate these connections and guarantee that you can make yourself clear serenely and obviously and, furthermore, accept the reactions.

Taking into account how significant communication is, it becomes important for you to master the art. That is, regardless of whether you are the most reserved individual with an unfortunate communication procedure, the standards I have framed here will cause an extraordinary improvement in your communication. Reading this book, you will:

- Find the ideal method for approaching anyone interestingly and making them like you.
- Know the genuine reasons you run out of comments during a discussion?

- Become sure about yourself while conversing with individuals (including outsiders) in every area of your life.
- Know how to keep up and maintain any conversation the right way
- Discover how you can stroll around a discussion when it turns out badly and put it back on the right track.

These methods are effective regardless of the individual(s) involved. And at the end of your journey reading this book, you will gain back every form of control you need during communication, both in your personal, social, and professional life.

Chapter 1. Speaking Skills

Have you ever had your knees and hands shake whenever you are standing in front of your audience? There will always come a time in your life wherein you have to expand your boundaries. There will be a time wherein you have to move from speaking to just one particular person, let us say your friend or your parent, to address a large group of people, let us say your entire classmate in your lecture class or the people in your work team. The idea is that talking to the public audience is inevitable.

But in the first place, why are we afraid of talking in public?

It may be because we think that people could not care less about what we will talk about. We feel like once we start speaking, they will just be yawning and be waiting for you to end your speech so they can have their freedom. Perhaps you've had a terrible event in the past when you were humiliated while speaking in public.

However, these should not hinder you from speaking yourself up. Now is the perfect time for you to know how you would enhance your skill in speaking and knock all your fears away.

Knock Your Fear Down

We know that your biggest enemy when it comes to speaking is fear. And when you fear, you hesitate.

You hesitate whenever you speak in front of an audience because you are unsure what you will say next. You may also start thinking that you are going to fail when you talk about this particular matter.

Usually, you are hesitant or nervous when you frequently say "um" or "er" or other fillers that are unnecessary to your speech. You may also be tripping over your own words from time to time because you are rushing to express your ideas as your brain works faster than your lips. Most of the time, speaking faster implies that you are nervous.

For you to be able to knock your hesitations, consider the following steps:

- **Think more clearly.** Doing this will help you focus on the particular matter that you are talking about, which will, in turn, make you speak clearly and well.

- **Slow down and emphasize your points.** It is not good to speak fast and stumble upon your words; this will only make your speech hard to understand. It's also crucial to highlight your main ideas so that your audience understands where you're going with your speech. This will also help you stay focused.

- **Breathe properly.** Proper breathing helps you stay relaxed. This will also keep you speak properly so that your audience will be able to understand you well.

When it comes to dealing with your nervousness, consider the following suggestions:

- **Do not make your nerves hinder you.** Do not always focus on yourself. Think about other speakers getting nervous too! But that is not the entire point. Just keep in mind that the people you are talking to are not aware of how nervous you are. There was a saying once that goes like this: "It is fine to have butterflies—as long as they fly in formation."

- **Connect with your audience.** The success of every communication flow depends on the effects on it the intended audience. Therefore, as the speaker, you must know the people you will talk to and connect with. Make sure that you know their current mood as you speak. If they are bored, make sure that you are lively to sort of wake them up.

- **Have your objectives in your mind.** You must know why you are speaking. Giving speeches is not only about disseminating information; it is also about engaging your audience and giving them what they need. Always keep in mind your objectives or the reason why you are speaking.

- **Be positive.** Always think about succeeding. Imagine yourself speaking confidently and clearly. Paint a picture of yourself talking without any flaws or mistakes. Always focus your mind on your desired outcome—what you want to achieve and not the things you do not like.

- **Relax.** Again, you must stay relaxed while you are speaking. Remove all the tensions, hesitations, and anything fearful in your system as you speak. Tell yourself with a smile that you are good enough.

Speak Up!

Judy Apps has also listed ten ways you would be able to speak with authority and charisma. Here's how:

When was the last time you heard someone talk with authority? With charisma? What were your thoughts while you listened? Did you feel like they are a very credible person with power and influence?

Speaking properly is probably one of the most common things that we want to achieve. We want to sound authoritative so that people will take us as confident and credible speakers. This will also make your audience pay more attention to you and what you are talking about because they find you influential and powerful.

Here are Apps' suggestions on how you would be able to improve your speaking skills:

1. **Stand with confidence.**

How you stand also affects how you speak. If you stand confidently, then you will most likely be able to speak confidently as well. People will also perceive you as confident since they can see you standing with poise; thus, they will give you their attention. Standing properly will also help you produce a better sound or voice while speaking.

You can improve your posture as you speak by finding your balance. Is your weight properly distributed between your feet so that you don't trip? Stand tall as well and keep your chin lifted. Doing so also adds to your height without any effort.

Moreover, you also have to relax (how many times have we already emphasized this point in this book? Oh well) and breathe. Release all the tension in your face, jaw, neck, and shoulders. Breathe out as well and let the air expand your entire body.

2. **Speak clearly.**

If you speak clearly and audibly, you will sound as if you mean what you are saying. It will sound like what you are saying comes from your heart. This will also help you engage your audience to listen to you because they understand what you are saying.

Open your mouth well as you speak, even though you are not that used to it. This may make you feel uneasy at first, but your audience may find it normal. Practice the mouth exercise as well. Make the vowel sounds more distinguishable and your consonants clearer as well.

3. Project properly.

Judy Apps suggests that people will most likely take you seriously if your voice has an impact on them. Therefore, you must project your voice according to the message you want to impose on your audience.

4. Emphasize your key points.

For you to be able to give your message to your audience clearly and effectively, you must emphasize your key points. This will let your audience know the important parts of your speech and give attention to you as you talk about these points. Also, there are times when other speakers give equal emphasis on every part of their speech, thus making it appear monotonous and boring. The sound is very flat, which in turn makes the listeners bored and feel sleepy. If you want to sound authoritative and charismatic, you have to emphasize strongly.

5. Do not rush.

How fast or slow you talk can affect the impression you make among other people. If you speak very fast, it may appear as if you are excited about talking about that particular subject matter. People may also think that you do not want to talk to them because you are rushing things. People may see you as dull if you talk slowly, and they will ultimately get weary of listening to you.

The point is that you have to monitor the speed of your speech. You neither have to talk fast or slowly; you have to keep it in moderation. Your speed may also vary, depending on what you are saying and the message you want to give to your audience. Again, you have to emphasize important points, so you should not give equal weight and speed to every part of your talk.

6. Use your instruments.

We are gifted with different instruments. It just depends on how we are going to use them to be able to speak properly.

You should also vary your pitch; keep your voice high or deep or anywhere in between, depending on your message. Use different volumes, wherein you have to speak loudly in some parts of your speech and softly in others. There are also some parts wherein you have to speak fast or slowly, depending on the points you want to emphasize.

7. Practice, practice, and practice.

If you're having trouble pronouncing a word, rehearse it so you won't have any trouble the next time you have to speak it.

Again, you just begin to hesitate while speaking because you happen to be unsure about what you will do and say next. If you will do a big speech about a particular subject matter, you must do your research to widen your knowledge about that topic. Then write your speech so that you know very well how it will go. And then practice delivering that speech for as much time as necessary.

"Practice makes perfect," as the adage goes.

8. Just be positive all the time.

You are the only one who can help you. If you imagine yourself succeeding, then you will most likely act towards achieving success.

Chapter 2. Why are Outstanding Conversation Skills Will Change Your Life?

Your communication abilities will determine your success no matter where you go, who you are, or what you want to do in life. You'll learn precisely what they do to attract others' attention thanks to this book. You may learn how to apply their methods for yourself, even if it seems to be magic!

It has already aided individuals of all ages and backgrounds, which I am pleased to report. I've been humbled by the wonderful comments I've gotten.

However, I felt there was space for a second book - one that would assist individuals improve their conversational abilities.

I'll teach you how to speak to anybody about anything and overcome social shyness in this tutorial. I won't sugarcoat it: developing your communication skills takes time and effort. It entails breaking lifelong habits and taking a few chances along the road. However, when you consider what you stand to earn, it's clear that you can't afford to allow any lack of communication skills become your greatest disadvantage. There are many advantages available to you:

1. Enhanced Career Prospects

Consider the steps you'll need to take to get a job, excel at your daily duties, establish relationships with your coworkers, and climb the corporate ladder. Your social skills must be excellent at every step, from the first interview through your first speech as a board member.

You won't be able to cooperate on projects if you can't communicate with your coworkers. You'll get a reputation as a bad communicator if you can't speak to your supervisor about any issues you're having at work. You get the picture - if you want to get that ideal job, you need to know how to conduct a conversation with anybody and everyone.

2. Better Business Relationships

One of the foundations of successful business partnerships is communication. You know how much of a barrier poor communication can be if you've ever had the misfortune of chatting with a drab person at a conference. You might be one of the greatest in your industry, but if you boring everyone you meet, you're unlikely to strike lucrative, mutually beneficial agreements and alliances.

3. Family Relationships

Contrary to popular belief, most family relationships aren't inherently simple, and many take a significant amount of effort.

You can only expect to create polite, loving family connections if you have learned the art of dispute resolution, know how to express your opinions without offending others, and know when to bite your tongue when required.

4. Better Romantic Relationships

This, along with my job issues, was one of the primary motivators for me to study communication skills. When I went on a date, I tried to be pleasant, humorous, and engaged. It took me a long time to understand that focusing on the other person is the key to having a good conversation. Even so, it's better to be late than never!

I'd like to believe I'm doing lot better in terms of romance these days. When you enhance your communication skills, whether you're a man or a woman, whether you're in a casual or more serious relationship, you can expect fewer arguments and better moments together.

5. Self-Esteem

Your self-esteem will be boosted by the friendships and business connections you form. We are social creatures that flourish when surrounded by others who embrace us and make us happy. As a result, we can develop our social abilities even more.

What is it about the art of communication that fascinates me? I didn't understand how much my social skills (or lack thereof) were limiting me until I was in my twenties.

Skeptical? It's time to consider a few erroneous ideas that may keep you trapped in the same old communication comfort zone. The first belief leads you to believe that communication isn't all that essential to begin with. The second promotes a fatalistic pessimism.

The Myth of the Socially Awkward Genius

Still, they comfort themselves by believing that there is a connection between a high IQ and an inability to conduct a good conversation.

Shows like The Big Bang Theory lead us to believe that very brilliant people are often socially awkward, but that this is irrelevant since they are incredibly intelligent in other ways.

This line of argument has two faults. The first is that there is no scientific evidence linking brilliance to poor social functioning. There are also a slew of specific instances that refute this notion. Albert Einstein, widely considered one of the world's most brilliant minds, was courteous and socially successful. 10 The second issue is that, even if there is a demonstrated negative connection between IQ and social ability, most of us are not geniuses.

Even if intellect were enough to ensure success in life, we couldn't get on it alone. This is a difficult reality for some of us to accept, given the fragile condition of the human ego. Fortunately, regardless matter whether you have a great intellect or not, you may learn to have successful social relationships with others.

Can Conversation and Social Skills Be Taught?

Suppose you've grown up with friends or family who have always done well in social situations. In that case, you may believe that social skills are something you're born with - you either can communicate with people in a variety of circumstances or don't. It's a sad idea, but the good news is that it's not true!

I know what it's like to be evaluated by others. Jason, my cousin, was always popular among his classmates, his instructors liked him, and almost every adult in our family adored him. If he hadn't been so courteous, I would have hated him. His mother always said that he was born with innate charm. Regrettably, her choice of words led me to think that charm and social ability were permanent characteristics.

Fortunately, I discovered that most individuals can improve if given the tools they need to assist themselves.

I believed I could improve my social skills after seeing how much of an effect they've had on so many people's lives. You have the option to alter your discussion, even if others have informed you that it is bland and useless. The greatest time to begin is right now!

Consider the treatments available to people with Asperger's Syndrome if you want further evidence that social skills can be taught (AS). Autism is a disease that affects a person's capacity to interact effectively with others. People with this diagnosis have a type of autism.

People with AS often talk incessantly about their hobbies, have trouble making eye contact, speak in a monotonous tone of voice, and show little interest in what others think or feel. Consequently, individuals often struggle to establish connections with others, which may lead to feelings of isolation and alienation from society.

The good news is that individuals with AS can be taught social skills, which may help them establish meaningful connections. Through role-play and training lead by trained therapists, they can learn how to "blend in" and function in most social settings.

What can we learn from this? The tale's lesson is clear: even if you have significant social skills deficiencies, you can learn how to connect with people if you are determined enough.

Finally, there's reason to think that you can learn to have excellent discussions, establish strong connections, and like being around other people at home and work. Even better, with practice, you'll become more accomplished.

It's important not to become too engrossed with the past. We've all been in uncomfortable situations and made social gaffes. That's perfectly typical! The most essential thing is to quit berating yourself for previous errors and prepare to alter how you interact with others.

Tips on How to Communicate Effectively

This will give you a few tips that can help you communicate in the best of ways. If you follow these suggestions, your communication skills will improve, and you will be able to have more enjoyable discussions with others around you.

Establish and Maintain Eye Contact

People often don't realize the importance of eye contact in communication. When you look at the other person while talking, you automatically build a great relationship that keeps the other person interested in the conversation. It tells the other person that you are into the conversation and makes an effort to get your point across to them in the best of ways. Imagine for a minute that you are in a classroom, and the teacher is talking to you. Would you be more interested in what she is saying if she looks at you and directs the conversation towards you? What if she turned her back on you and started writing on the blackboard while she was still speaking to you? That's your answer right there. When a person makes eye contact while talking, you can see the person's expressions, and you are much better able to understand what the other person is saying.

Eye contact also acts as a synchronizing signal most of the time. People look up after they finish a sentence to see what the other person thinks and see whether or not they give relevant feedback. At the end of grammatical breaks, too, people look up to get feedback and try to make their point in the best of ways. According to a source, a lack of eye contact can also signal that the other person is embarrassed or that there is no clarity in their thoughts. Research shows that people look at each other 75% of the time when they are talking and around 40% when they are listening. It also greatly depends on the personality traits of a person. People who are extroverts and are generally friendlier tend to look up more amidst a conversation and try to make eye contact.

The importance of eye contact in body language cannot be overstated. Research shows that to have the right kind of communication, appropriate body language is important.

Frequently, our body language is known to speak more than our words and is the topmost factor that keeps the audience engaged. There is a famous saying that goes, "eyes are a reflection of your inner self." This saying is very apt in this context. Your eyes reveal a lot about you, and making eye contact allows you to communicate more effectively with the other person.

Send a Clear Message

When you simply try to say something, the message might not go to the other person as intended. When you make a conscious effort to say something with the right kind of intention, your message is understood well. When you are clear with your message, you can get your point across when you choose your words wisely. Keeping the communication objective in mind is the best thing to do. You must ask yourself what you are attempting to accomplish. When you know the answer to this, you need to make sure that you make the right choice of words to understand your point. If you choose words that might even have the slightest chances of distorting the message, you might not get the message across clearly, which can hamper effective communication. Just make sure that you understand the audience well and then choose the kind of words you should go for. Also, it is always beneficial to go for simpler words since that can ensure that your message is understood clearly. The use of jargon only hampers effective communication. For the other person to best understand what you're trying to say, you should choose words that are easy to understand. You need to be very clear with what you're saying so that there's no way for your message to be misinterpreted. The entire point of communicating with the other person is that they understand what you say to them and try to make sense of it in the context you want them to. That is ideally what your aim should be. To convey your message in the best way, it is essential to choose your words wisely.

Be Receptive

When you are on the listening end of a conversation, make sure that your gestures and body language are so that the other person also enjoys making conversation with you. When you are receptive, you give off a signal to the other person that tells them that you are interested, and that way, they will make more effort to get their point across to you. It all boils down to active listening. If the speaker is saying something that you don't understand, make sure to stop them there and then tell them that you don't understand what they are saying to adapt accordingly and engage in a productive conversation. There is no point in actually making conversation with another person when you and the speaker are not able to understand each other. While the other person is speaking, make sure you nod or smile to know that you are interested in what they are saying. Even if you think that you are not interpreting the information clearly or in the right way just like the speaker wants you to, make sure that you make a conscious effort to at least try to understand. The speaker will feel very satisfied when you do that, and that will increase the chances of you both being in a useful conversation.

Wait For the Other Person to Finish

Most people like to be on the speaking end and want the other person to listen. They don't even let the other person finish, and they interrupt them and start speaking out of turn. This doesn't give off a good message to the other person. When they see that you are not interested in the conversation, they also lose interest, and then there is no point in the conversation. You should always carefully listen to the other person when they are speaking. This also shows a lot of respect and shows the other person that you are interested in saying. Always remember that this is a matter of giving and taking. When you engage in active listening when the other person is talking, they will listen to what you are saying carefully. That way, it will be a respectful conversation, and both parties will understand each other, and the message will go out just as intended.

When both parties listen to each other, they care and are respectful towards each other. Most people who are self-obsessed are also known to keep talking about themselves to the other person. They genuinely feel that they are more interesting than the other person. Other people who have a shy personality are known to be overwhelmed by their feelings, and these people are not comfortable when talking about themselves. It is important to note here that monologues are never a good thing, and they send a really wrong message to the listener. This is why it is really important to engage in a two-way conversation. Two-way conversations get people closer and are much more likely to be successful conversations.

To feel included in a conversation, it's generally best to wait until the other person has finished speaking. Some people are generally impatient and cannot wait to get their points across. It is always recommended to inculcate this habit in yourself to wait it out and wait for the other person to finish speaking. Once the other person is done with putting forward his point to you, then you should put forward your point so that both parties can understand each other in the best of ways. The importance of effective communication should never be underestimated. Often, people in high management positions like doctors or politicians are great speakers, but they don't let others finish. Even to people like that, it is recommended that they first hear the other person out and then communicate their point of view.

If you keep these points of view in mind, you will much better engage in effective communication. Believe me; you will see the difference in no time. Simply keep these ideas or points in mind if you're attempting to strike up a conversation with someone.

Chapter 3. Communication Skills

Good communication skills are essential if you and others want to understand information faster and more accurately.

Improve Communication Skills

1. Listening

Being an effective communicator necessitates being a good listener. Active listening is important – pay attention to what others say and clarify ambiguities by rephrasing your questions for better understanding.

2. Conciseness

Transmit your message as quickly as possible. Avoid unnecessary words and go right to the point. Rambling will make the listener smooth or uncertainon what you say. Don't talk too much, and don't use words that can confuse the audience.

3. Confidence

Be sure of what you say and your interactions with others. Confidence can be as easy as eye contact, a relaxed body stance, and concision talking. Avoid using angry or demeaning noises, and avoid making comments that seem like inquiries.

4. Open-mindedness

If you disagree with what another person has to say, whether it's an employer, a colleague, or a friend, it's important to sympathize with their views rather than simply trying to get your message across. Respect others' opinions and never degrade those who do not agree with you.

5. Using the correct medium

There are many means of communication – choosing the right one is crucial. For example, it is more important to speak in person about serious matters (relays, wage adjustments, etc.) than to send an email about the matter.

Great Career

Strong communication skills can help you to get through an interview and the selection process. The ability to communicate well is a huge asset! To perform your work well, you must be able to solve problems, request information, communicate with people, and have excellent interpersonal contact - all of which need solid communication skills. They allow you to be well known and to understand your needs.

Bad Communication in the Workplace

Communication drives productivity in the workplace. While the downside of bad communication with others may not be evident in the short term, it has a detrimental impact on the workplace in the long term.

Chapter 4. Career Success

Career success is achieved through effective communication skills. An individual's success in any profession can be attributed to the extent to which he/she can use communication skills effectively. Skills like listening, speaking in public, controlling emotions, giving presentations, group discussions, and writing formal letters, memos, documents, articles, and stories are necessary.

Communication skills are important in all walks of life. They indeed play a vital role in organizational leadership, personal development, and in life. No matter how big the army of employees is, how big the organization is or how much the salary they are drawing, they are useless without effective communication skills.

Communication skills are vital in project management, marketing, sales, or personnel management. They are indeed essential if you are going to climb the corporate ladder. They are also as important at home. Effective communication skills can help you bond better with your family and small children. Research has proven that parents can bond better with their children with effective communication skills.

Basic skills and training is available to people at many places. These skills are referred as basic communication skills. These basic communication skills are essential as they help establish a bond with people. Effective communication skills are vital if you are to establish a relationship with anyone. It is nothing but the way you sell yourself to someone. It is your emotional appeal. It is nothing but building rapport with people.

Effective communication skills are appreciated at the workplace. People realize the need for communication skills in the workplace. Professionalism, loyalty, and commitment are some common terms used for effective communication skills. One can be emotionally stable and with good boundaries, if they have effective communication skills.

One with excellent communication skills can be a mentor to people. Mentor coaching or leadership training is available as a course of study. Employers seek employees with communication skills. The first impression is the last. Employers feel that employees with excellent communication skills can bring in more business.

The credibility of the employees is established with effective communication skills. Employees are assured that they can meet their job requirements if they have excellent communication skills. Effective communication skills help them build confidence and rapport in the workplace.

People with effective communication skills can present their ideas and proposals with confidence. Effective communication skills eliminate this problem of rejection or feeling ignored. People realize that they are liked and accepted.

The effectiveness of communication skills also depends greatly on the nature of the group we are addressing. For instance, people from the corporate world are different from the government bureaucracy. We may face people with a negative approach. If this is so, our communication skills should be different. Effective communication skills help you cope with the situation.

Effective communication skills help you develop rapport with people, including bosses and subordinates, customers, parents, and wives. Effective communication skills bring confidence and satisfaction to the workplace. Effective communication skills are the key to success.

Now, let us discuss the importance of communication skills in personal life. Communication skills also help us in our relationships. Effective communication skills help us bond better with our family members. Effective communication skills help us connect better with our children. Effective communication skills create unity in the family. Effective communication skills help us bring harmony to our family. Effective communication skills create cooperation.

Chapter 5. Start a Conversation with Anyone

Imagine that you are at a conference, party, or even the local park and you see someone that you want to talk with. It can be someone you noticed for the first time, a potential client for your business, or someone you have a romantic interest in. You can either maintain your distance and avoid the person entirely or take the initiative to strike up a conversation with them. This probably sounds simple, but in that instance, do you know what to say to this person? Do you start worrying that you don't know what to talk about? Does thinking about all this give you anxiety and scare you from even making the first move?

You don't need to be in this situation ever again. You can start a conversation with anyone and at any time. You can also do this gracefully.

Rapport Across the Room

You can build rapport with others without even saying a word. It can be something as simple as a reciprocated smile or even eye contact. When you acknowledge someone's presence before approaching and talking to them, it makes the conversation easier to start.

It also goes a long way in making the introduction much easier than it would have been without the rapport. For instance, if there is someone you admire at the party, you make eye contact with them and if it is reciprocated, why don't you go ahead and introduce yourself? This rapport essentially acts as a cue to start the conversation.

One thing you must understand is just because you are trying to build a rapport across the room it doesn't mean everyone is going to flock to you. It still means you'll have to make a little effort and initiate the conversation.

Mindset Matters

Your mindset matters in all aspects of life and starting a conversation with someone is not an exception. Having the right mindset makes it easier to start a conversation with a stranger. When starting a conversation with a stranger, your thoughts consider all the unknown variables. Such thoughts simply increase fear and make you hesitant.

The simplest way to actually change your mindset is to let go of any worrying thoughts that bring you down when you are trying to approach someone. One thing you should not forget in life is that unless you take a risk you will not get a reward. If you are worried that the person you have approached will give you the cold shoulder or will reject you, ask yourself, "What is the worst that will happen?" It might mean you will not get to have a conversation with them. That's likely the worst-case scenario.

Common Ground

One of the known best ways to start a conversation is by identifying a common interest or trait. This is an icebreaker that makes it easier to start conversing. If you notice something in common with a stranger, use it as an opening line. Perhaps it is an article of clothing that supports a sports team that you like, a tattoo on their body, or it could also be a specific brand of the clothing. You can use it to start a conversation.

A conversation that starts with a similar interest or is based on shared interests is more engaging. It also increases the chances of establishing a genuine connection with the other person. Remember that the world is filled with different people who have varying ideas and opinions. So, look for some common ground and base the conversation around it.

A Common Topic Helps

A straightforward yet effective means to start a conversation with anyone is to comment on a common topic. It probably sounds silly but it is effective. There are several things that you share in common with the other person when you exist in the same space. The most common topics you can start talking about include the weather and traffic. Is it extremely hot? Is the weather frosty and unbearably cold? Perhaps it's been raining endlessly? Or maybe it's a beautiful day out there! Whatever it is, you can start a conversation by sharing your delight or frustration about the weather conditions. Do not shift into a full-blown technical mode and explain the weather. Instead, it should just be a passing comment. Chances are the person you are trying to talk to will reciprocate and reply.

For instance, those living in a metropolitan city are usually frustrated about the traffic conditions. This topic of traffic can be a conversation starter. Maybe you can share a secret shortcut or two that bypasses some of the traffic. Make the most of this opportunity and say something about it. Apart from this, simply look around your environment and look for something common you share with this stranger. Whether it is a beautiful garden or a child playing recklessly, you can simply comment about this and initiate a conversation. That said, ensure that the situation is apt before you try to initiate a conversation. For instance, if someone seems to be in a hurry to get somewhere and you are trying to initiate a conversation about the weather, it will backfire.

Concentrate on Something Pleasant

If you are struggling to find something meaningful to talk about, then focus on something pleasant. For instance, if you are actually at a party, saying something as simple as, "Wow, this is a great turnout for this event," or "These canapés taste amazing," can do the trick! Saying something negative might initiate a conversation but it is too risky. For instance, you are at a conference and start a conversation with someone new by saying, "that keynote address was too boring." However, it turns out the person you just told this to is the keynote speaker's partner. To avoid getting embroiled in controversies and to ensure you do not start a conversation on the wrong foot, avoid any criticism as a conversation starter.

Ask for Assistance

In some situations, asking for assistance from someone else can also be a conversation starter. Whether it is help reaching a top shelf or asking someone to help find something you misplaced. However, it is unlikely that you have such situations in all scenarios. If an opportunity presents itself, go ahead and take it. It's okay to ask others for help. Ensure that your request is genuine and something you cannot do. Similarly, you can also offer assistance if you see someone struggling. Once again this might not be applicable in all situations but offering assistance, especially to someone you are keen on talking to, is a great chance. Before you ask or offer assistance, ensure that you are not excessive or intrusive. If it looks like you have eavesdropped or pushed yourself into an ongoing conversation, it will backfire.

Develop Confidence

How you present yourself matters because it determines how others respond to you. When you exude confidence, it becomes easier for others to talk to you. This can be the most challenging aspect of initiating a conversation because you might not feel confident. You're probably wondering how others will respond to you, whether your approach is right, or if you are saying the right things. These thoughts can quickly erode your self-confidence. On the other hand, when you exude self-confidence, it shows you are in control of the situation. If you doubt your worth or think you are uninteresting, then it is time to fix this. The simplest means to do this is by taking some time for self-introspection and making a note of different reasons why you are an interesting person. If you think you don't have any exciting stories to share, why don't you look for something from the past that shows you are interesting. Understand that you are worth talking to. If you think you are uninteresting or that you are not worth it, others will also sense it. It is okay to have setbacks and weaknesses but not playing to your strengths is a mistake.

- In order to improve your communication skills, you will need to ensure that you can comfortably start a conversation with anyone.

- Being able to start a conversation with anyone will allow you to meet new people, network with others, strengthen bonds, and build meaningful relationships.

- The key to starting a conversation is to not overthink the situation and to simply focus on commonalities (e.g. ask them a question that they can easily answer, comment on a sports team that they are brandishing on their shirt, comment on something happening at the event your both attending, etc.)

Chapter 6. Different People, Different Approach

Recently, I was delivering a talk on advanced communication skills. The subject of body language came up. One attendee asked if body language varies between different personalities. I thought this was a great question because indeed it does.

You can learn a lot about somebody, and their personality type, just by looking at their body language and nonverbal communication. Let's look at some personality types.

Personality Types

Personality types have been around for a long time. Hippocrates called these the four temperaments. He established the four archetypes of people's personalities. This has evolved.

This relies on filling in a questionnaire to identify the different types. While this information is useful, it is just not practical to give a questionnaire to someone and then ask them to fill it in. We need a method where we can use our observational and awareness skills instead. This is where our understanding of body language and nonverbal communication will serve us well.

Identifying a Personality

My favoured method is the Merrill-Wilson model. It is simple to understand and fast to identify. The four personality types are Dominant, Expressive, Amiable, and Analytical. There are two main variables to identify a personality type. Are they better with either facts & data or relationships? Are they introverted (low assertion) or extroverted (high assertion)?

From this, we get four main types:

Dominant – Fact-Based, Extrovert, High Emotional Control

Analytical – Fact-Based, Introvert, High Emotional Control

Amiable – Relationship-Based, Introvert, Low Emotional Control

Expressive – Relationship-Based, Extrovert, Low Emotional Control

People will move between these boxes in different situations and can be any of the four, but will feel more comfortable in one. The archetype that people actually fall into is easy to recognise once we know what to look for. This can be useful when dealing with people. It can give you an indication when communicating with them and selecting which type of strategy to adopt.

The Clues

The first step is to identify whether somebody is an introvert or an extrovert. Having done that, then pay attention to the warmth of the greeting that you get. This will actually give you an indication of whether emotional thinking will influence decisions or not.

Dominant - Aim to be in control

Dominant people exhibit control and power. They often display a firm handshake, direct eye contact and controlled body language with little blinking of the eyes. Expect to see strong eye contact that can sometimes be a little uncomfortable. They will often use the dominant handshake where the knuckles are facing upwards and the palm faces downward. The body language reflects control and dominance and they don't move much. When they move, it is with purpose. They often place their hands on their hips to make themselves bigger. Body positions include standing upright to appear taller with their head back. Sometimes they may sit with their hands behind their head in an outstretched position. These people often like to play power games, which will include having a larger desk or being more elevated than the person with whom they are meeting. To demonstrate control, they may swivel the chair to the side or even with their back facing you. This all illustrates the power and control that they perceive they have.

Early in my sales career, I remember visiting a dominant in his office. He took the whole control aspect a stage further. I was young at the time and was fazed by his behaviour. Not only did he swivel his seat around with his back facing me, but he also did so while eating a bacon roll (a loose equivalent to a bagel if you are from the US). This was beyond dominance. It was rude. I was young, and didn't have the confidence to pull him up on it. At parties, dominants like to make an impressive entrance. They tend not to smile, as this is perceived as a sign of weakness.

When they laugh in public, it is in a very controlled way. They like other people to come up to them. They are often in the centre of the room, surrounded by people of lower status. The people of lower status will exhibit lower status non-verbal signals, such as lowering of the head.

Expressive - Aim to be noticed

Expressives often greet people with a warm greeting and display an enthusiastic handshake. They are less formal. They are friendly and warm but are not afraid to say no. They have less control over their body language and it is very expressive. They are animated when they speak. Expect to see palm gestures as they use their arms and hands to communicate their excitement. There is often a higher degree of lower body movement. Expressives move a lot and tend to blink a lot, too. Decisions are based on emotion. Expect to see a lot of comfortable eye contact.

They are not overbearing and eye contact moves around a lot. When seated, expressives will often take up a lot of space and often in some unusual seated positions. As their attention span is very low, they are easily distracted and display signs of distraction. Expressives enjoy things that are exciting and new. Expect to see displays of boredom or disinterest if they don't agree with you. They smile a lot and are not afraid to laugh. At parties, expressives are usually the centre of attention and at the hub of what is going on. They like to make a grand entrance acknowledging everyone as they come into the room.

Amiable - Aim to blend in

Amiables are introverts. They aim to please and dislike confrontation and will often see both sides of the argument. They will often greet with a soft handshake. They are trusting and want everyone to get along. Their body language reflects being introverted, and they tend to make themselves smaller and less conspicuous. They do this by keeping their arms and legs under control and close to the body. They are literally making themselves less noticeable. Their head is often down in a slightly lowered position to avoid being noticed. Amiables hate confrontation and do not display strong eye contact. They don't like confrontation or being pressurised. Signs of discomfort are often displayed if pressure is applied to them. They tend to move slower and with controlled movement. At parties, amiables are often at the side of the room. This ties in with not wanting to be noticed. They are often involved in a conversation not with a group of people but with another person on a one-to-one basis. When they smile, it is more of a warm smile and when they laugh, it is more controlled. When an amiable enters the room, they aim to do so without being noticed.

Analytical - Aim to work things out

Analyticals love data, details and spreadsheets. They often walk with their head leaning forwards. These people are introverted and very often have very low external awareness. They have very poor eye contact and tend to look down a lot when they speak to you. They have a high degree of emotional control and can give the impression that they are not interested in what somebody else is saying. This comes from their lack of understanding of how to engage. As they have low self-awareness skills, they will sometimes wear some unusual clothes that don't quite fit in with the occasion. Their low awareness skills can also be observed with their lack of facial expressions that reflect the different emotions in a story that someone may be telling. They tend not to smile a lot. This can give the impression of being aloof and unengaged. Fig. 3 summarises the different personality types.

Changing Styles

Using this analysis of body language enables us to adapt our style when engaging with other people. If, for example, we meet an amiable, we would know that we would need to adapt our style. They enjoy reassurance and like things at a slow pace. Trust is very important to them. If you are dealing with an expressive ask them about their holiday expect and them to talk a lot. They will be very open with information and will be more than happy to talk enthusiastically and expressively. If you are dealing with a dominant, expect to keep the relationship professional and to get to the point fairly quickly. Dominants like to challenge people. Expect to be challenged and to know everything about your subject. If you are dealing with an analytical, expect to find it difficult to have much of a conversation with them. Everything is based on logic and process. They would expect you to explain what you are doing and to know all the technical details, including all the micro details, if you are asked. These people dislike generalisation and disorganisation. Expect them to turn up on time. They will expect you to turn up on time, too.

Chapter 7. How to Avoid Being Rude When Talking with Someone

Many social situations require that you be courteous. There is little to be gained from coming off as harsh, whether you are establishing a lasting friendship with a friend or meeting someone for the first time. The majority of rudeness is, regrettably, unintentional and the result of miscommunication and a lack of self-awareness. One thing is to be courteous. Another is not being impolite. Thankfully, negative social habits may be changed if you find yourself in a situation where you may have given the wrong impression to someone. The first step in enhancing your presentation style is becoming aware of it.

Speaking with Politeness

Before you talk, think. If more consideration were put into it, so many social blunders could be prevented. A person with true conversational talent will always attempt to filter his words before speaking them. Even while planning out every word you'll say may seem mentally taxing to some, it doesn't actually take much brainpower. Really, all it actually takes is a split second to decide whether something you say might be hurtful to someone around. It's preferable to hold your tongue for the time being if you don't feel well about speaking something.

Be aware of your voice. Being aware of how you sound when you speak might be beneficial. While concentrating on oneself during a discussion might be distracting, paying attention to the tone, tempo, and loudness of your voice can help you avoid unintended rudeness.

- Pay close attention to how quickly you speak. When under pressure, those who are jittery or uneasy have a tendency to speak more quickly. This merely makes the situation more unpleasant.

Empathize with others in your conversation. In a conversation, empathy can benefit you much. Not the least of the advantages is being respected for manners and consideration. Almost everyone possesses empathy to some degree. Being genuinely interested in actually what the other person is saying is the key to drawing it out.

Make a conscious effort to understand someone else's perspective while they are sharing details of their lives with you. Try to understand how that could feel, for example, if he recently lost his job. It is simpler to charm empathic folks since they are aware of other people's sentiments.

- Even in unpleasant conversations, empathy can be effective. Speaking with someone who is hostile or vindictive can be frustrating. While it may be easy to lash out at someone like that, empathy might help you maintain composure. Consider the problem from the perspective of the unpleasant individual. In some instances, stepping outside of your own perspective for a little while can provide you a fresh perspective on the circumstance.

- Before you lash out at someone you believe is being impolite to you, take a deep breathe and inquire, "Hey, what's going on?" or "What's going on here?"

Ignore rumors. An easy path to rudeness is through gossip. Nobody enjoys being discussed. Many people find it offensive to hear about people they know negatively, even if the subject in question isn't present to hear it.

You should avoid conversations like these if you don't want to act rudely yourself. Turn the other cheek even if some are slandering others. Those who are present when you reject the offer will see you favorably as a result.

Remain humble. For almost all polite individuals, modesty is a virtue. Some people are impolite because they put too much emphasis on themselves. The majority of the time, this is a mistake that is readily avoidable by attempting to listen to both sides of the debate.

Allow the other speaker to finish. Even if everything you say is true, if you don't consider the other person's perspective, you'll still come across as impolite. People generally prefer to express their opinions. If they are unable to speak, they will feel restricted.

- This can be communicated through mild answers like nodding your head or by just restating the main points of what the other person said.

Being Mindful of the Other Person

Up your politeness game. Depending on who you are spending time with, different people will have different expectations for manners or etiquette. When all else fails, it's a good idea to read up on correct etiquette. Even though the concept of "good manners" is connected with the archaic Victorian era, many of the traditions are still relevant today. It is preferable to follow a custom than to ignore it if you are even the slightest bit hesitant. No less necessary now than it was then, politeness has new guidelines that should be followed in contemporary society.

- General, avoid looking at your phone while speaking to someone.

- Give the other person enough time to complete their sentence.

- Never forget to express your politeness and gratitude. Over the years, these tricks have never fallen out of favor.

Consider the sensibilities of the other person. Talking to someone who is naturally sensitive makes it even harder to avoid coming across as unpleasant. In most cases, emotional sensitivity should be regarded favorably, but it can be challenging when speaking with someone who might be upset by the smallest offense. Before engaging in a lengthy chat with someone if you believe this to be the case, it is a good idea to be aware of their particular preferences. For instance, it's advisable to wait to use vulgar humor around someone if you believe they won't find it amusing while you're around.

- Discover their preferences or emotional triggers by asking them. If that doesn't work, it's usually a good idea to observe someone in a social setting before you interact with them.

Determine the other person's emotional state. Even though it doesn't need any action on your behalf, empathy and understanding how the other person is feeling while you're talking can help you fully avoid being unpleasant in many situations. Your best actual course of action is to attempt to determine how they are feeling through non-verbal cues because people may be complicated in this regard. Make it a habit to observe someone's expression while they are speaking. Sometimes what they say will not match the tone that their look suggests.

- Unfortunately, most people won't honestly answer the question "How are you feeling" when asked. People aren't taught to accurately describe their emotions.

Others can be reluctant to express their actual emotions or feel embarrassed.

Consider cultural differences. What someone deems to be disrespectful often reflects the culture in which they were reared. It's a good idea to familiarize yourself with what is and isn't proper in their eyes if you're going to be traveling or dealing with people who were raised in different cultures on a daily basis. The simple act of researching these practices in advance will be considered as exceedingly gracious on your behalf, even if people are normally used to getting past these cultural differences.

Adjust your behavior to the situation. The conditions of your scenario must be taken into account before acting, as is the case with the majority of social encounters. In other words, your manners will vary based on whether you're at a wedding, a funeral, or just a regular night out. Being polite entails having self-awareness and tact. Behaving upbeat at a wake for a deceased person will have the same unfavorable effects as acting down at a birthday party.

- This should also apply to how you dress and look. People will make a lot of judgments about you depending on how you present yourself.

- When in doubt about how to behave in a social situation, it's a good idea to try imitating what other people are typically doing.

Be courteous at all times. You can't rely on politeness for the short term if you want to be perceived as someone who is truly tactful and nice. Being polite cannot be an act. Instead, it must be a persistent frame of mind. Be constant in your actions. Someone will perceive you as being even more fake if they see two different sides of you.

Utilizing Proper Body Language

Copy the expression on the other person's face. You might occasionally be unsure about how to behave or respond to someone. You can show that you and the other person are on the same page by mirroring each other's expression. The majority of the time, this will be seen favorably.

- If you believe the other person is using sarcasm, it is not advisable to imitate him.

Maintain a high standard of hygiene. If the fundamentals aren't taken care of initially, even the most charitable person can come out as harsh. This entails showering at least a couple times per week and ensuring sure your clothing is clean. You won't likely make any friends and people are sure to find you repulsive if you always have a bad body odor. In terms of etiquette, something this simple can make all the difference.

Keep your blinking in check. When they're stressed out, some people have a tendency to blink quickly. If the other person notices, it may appear to them that you're hurried or uncomfortable. It can be challenging to stop doing this unintentionally, let alone even recognize when you do it. Try to be aware of your blinking the next time you're in a moderately stressful scenario.

- By giving yourself permission to relax, you can lessen one aspect of negative body language as well as others.

When you're stressed out, pay additional attention to your body language. Most of the time, body language is performed automatically. We can frequently tell when we're stressed out by the way our bodies are arranged. Even if we try to be as courteous as possible in other situations, this rudeness still manages to get through. The easiest way to manage it is to put a lot of emphasis on being aware of your own body language. Crossed arms and an aggressive stance may come easily, but by concentrating on how your body is responding, you can prevent these symptoms of stress from manifesting.

Chapter 8. How to Build Confidence

Building up your confidence is the first step to being able to speak to anyone. The trick is to start feeling confident before you actually become confident. This might sound silly, but sometimes we really do have to fake it until we make it. This is not in a bad way. We have to just feel what it is like to be confident before our inner confidence starts to build up. The tips below are all about making yourself feel more confident. You will actually feel the difference when you do these things. You might also notice that other people think you are more confident, and they will want to talk to you first. Try these out and see if anything changes in the way you feel and the way other people interact with you.

Take Care of Your Body

It is very rare to actually find someone who works out, eats healthy, and takes care of their body yet feels self-conscious. If you think about it, you only ever take care of things that have some sort of value. You would never take care of something that you deem as unimportant. When you take the time to care for your body and your needs, you are telling yourself that you are worth something and have value. This subconsciously makes you more confident.

Small changes matter when it comes to self-care. You only need a few actual minutes a day to do this, but they are definitely worth it. When I say schedule, I mean it. Make an appointment with yourself and actually mark it on your calendar. This communicates that this time is important to you, and you are going to make it a priority.

Watch What Your Body is Saying

Our body language speaks volumes, both to others and to ourselves. People will see what your body is portraying before they actually come up to speak to you. If you look timid and shy, then most of the time, people will skip over you because they think that you want to be alone. The way you carry yourself also affects the way you feel about yourself. Simply changing the way you sit or stand can have a massive impact on how you feel. You might feel a little uncomfortable with doing the things that I am going to mention, but they are not hard at all. Push through the discomfort. It is just there because you are not used to carrying yourself in this way.

The first thing that you have to consider is your posture. Being slouched and hunched over makes you smaller and makes you feel smaller. It closes you off to the rest of the world. When you sit up, roll your shoulders back, and keep your head upright you are communicating to the world that you are open and confident. The next thing that you have to do is watch your hands. If you have them crossed all the time, it shows that you are closed off. It is also a way to protect yourself, so when you do this, you do not feel comfortable or confident in the situation you are in. Rather leave them to hang to your sides, rest on a table or object next to you, place them on your lap, or hold something.

You should also make sure that you put your phone away. Many times we just pick up our phones so that it looks like we are busy. This is a defense mechanism because we don't want to look like we are alone or we want to distract ourselves. This does not show confidence, and it can close you off to other people.

Everything about your body language should communicate openness and confidence. Be aware of how you are standing and even what your face is communicating. Many of us have a resting face that is not the friendliest. Every few minutes, do a quick internal scan of yourself to check what your body and face are doing. You can make adjustments as necessary so that you present yourself as more friendly and feel more confident.

Start Repeating Some Positive Affirmations

When you start to speak to yourself in a more positive way, you will start to feel more confident. A lot of the things that make us feel insecure are things that we say to ourselves. If you were to think back to all the mean or negative things that were said to you by other people and then compare it to the number of negative things you think and say to yourself, you would probably notice that the latter is a whole lot more. This is because we tend to be harder on ourselves than what is necessary. We hold such a high standard for ourselves and then beat ourselves up when we do not get there.

This is a very unhealthy way of living and treating ourselves. When we start to change that and start speaking more positively, it changes us. What we listen to will affect the way we feel and act. This is why it is so important to make sure that you are always watching what you think and say to yourself.

The best way to make sure that you are saying something positive is to have a list of positive affirmations that you repeat to yourself. This will make sure that you have something on hand. Sometimes the negative thoughts just creep in, and we need to have a positive saying to counteract that.

Start thinking about all the negative things that you usually think to yourself. If you find that you constantly think that you are not good enough, you can counter that with a saying like, "I am worthy," "I have already accomplished so much and can do it again," or "I am capable of doing this." This will help to shift your focus, and it will allow you to be more positive.

You could also have a list of positive affirmations that you repeat to yourself in the morning. This will allow you to start your day off on a positive note. You will be much better equipped to fend off any negative thoughts and feelings of not being confident. All it takes is actually about five minutes in the morning, and you will be able to see the difference.

Dress Confidently

If you eventually look at some of the most confident people in the world, this would be public speakers, actors, and high-powered executives, they all dress well. They may not all dress the same, but they dress in a way that makes them feel confident.

I have seen that most people choose to dress for comfort. There is nothing bad about being comfortable, but when you dress in a way that just serves the purpose of comfort, then you are not going to portray confidence to the world and, as a result, won't feel confident. Dressing more confidently is probably going to take you out of your comfort zone. This is a good thing. When you dress better, people will notice, and that starts to build up your confidence.

I would suggest that you first start out simply. Pick colors that are neutral because they go with everything, and it is really difficult to go wrong with them. Colors like black, white, grey, and brown go with everything and agree with everyone. If you are a guy, you can choose simple jeans, button-down shirts, dress pants, and grab a pair of really nice shoes. For a lady, you can choose a simple black dress, jeans, button-down shirts, slacks, and heels are also great for confidence. It also depends on your lifestyle, certain things might not be appropriate for certain settings, but the point is that you make an effort in the way you dress.

This comes back to the point of taking care of yourself. When you spend a little extra time on yourself to make sure that you look good, then you have placed value on yourself. This automatically conveys that you see value in who you are, and that is why you choose to invest your time and energy in yourself. It might actually take some time to get used to if you are the type of person who doesn't really give a second thought to the clothes that you wear, but it is definitely worth it. The more you do it, the better you will become at picking clothes that make you feel confident. You can actually also look at YouTube for some videos on smart and confident dressing. This way, you will get some visual ideas and can build up from there.

Chapter 9. Public Speaking

A public talk is essentially an oral presentation or lecture delivered to a live audience. For the most part, it is a formal or planned event, while spontaneous speeches are common and may be a distinguishing professional trait. On the other side, you may be sitting in an executive meeting believing you're just there to observe when you're asked to expound on a component of the supporting research and investigation or to protect your ideas.

Public Speaking Importance

What is public speaking, if not a dressed-up (or not, depending on your audience) version of the fundamental talents we've been using since we first began defining desires and sculpting the words and gestures to convey those desires?

Ok, life back then was simple; a youngster is pointing and approaching a bowl of grapes, or a baby drinking more milk till they had what they needed. Of course, one critical dynamic has remained constant. If you don't ask, you don't receive. This is true in general and in specific expertly. If you need the transaction, contract, finance, position, assignment, or progress, you must be prepared and ready to make a legitimate and persuasive request. Normally, you'll have to do so in front of a group of deciders who will determine the response to your request.

Public speaking is also a unique and cost-effective way to improve your image and organization within your organization, calling, or industry, as well as perhaps raise funds for your organization locally. Public speaking removes you and your argument from the general clamor, whether you're promoting a product, administration, idea, organization, or person (including yourself). Public speaking, as professional speakers and innovators point out, is a kind of worship.

The general public expects you to be an expert on the subject since you're speaking about it. The image people get of you is based on the content of your speech, but just being a speaker gives you a level of credibility that would need some effort to establish in any case. Talking allows you to establish a reputation as a potential pioneer of local pioneer, increasing your visibility and market value. Even if it makes it via the channels, that is unlikely to happen with an introduction letter, CV, or pitch.

The Listeners Expectations

Consideration is one of the nicest and most unusual gifts a person can offer. That gift comes with an expectation when it comes to the audience's attention. Crowd assumptions supplement the three presenter inspirations. Individuals in the audience, in particular, desire to benefit from an informative speech, be inspired by an inspiring discourse or be energized by a helpful discourse.

Ask Attention of the Audience Before Speaking

When you speak, make an effort to pull in your audience. As a result, you'll feel less alone as a speaker, and everyone will be aware of your message. Pose driving questions if it's appropriate. People or groups are assigned to them, and they are encouraged to participate and ask questions. Keep in mind that several words might detract from your strength as a speaker. Consider the following sentences: "I certainly must add that I believe we can reach these goals" or "I just believe this setup is a good one." The phrases "just" and "I believe" restrict your conviction and authority. It's best not to use them.

"Really," as in "Really, I'd like to emphasize that we were below budget last quarter," is a comparative word. When you say "truly," it conveys a sense of acceptance or perhaps surprises. If everything else is equal, say what things are. "Last quarter, we stayed under budget," says the executive. Also, pay attention to how you speak. If you're nervous, you may speak quickly. This increases your chances of stumbling over your words or saying something you don't intend. By taking deep breaths, you may force yourself to slow down. Don't be hesitant to collect your thoughts; pauses are an important part of the conversation, and they help you seem confident, regular, and genuine.

Finally, try not to read from your notes in precisely the same terms. Make a list of essential points on rapid cards, or try to recall what you will say as you become better at public speaking. You can always go back to your suggestion cards when you need them.

Importance of Body Language in Public Speaking

In case you weren't aware, your nonverbal communication is very important. It will send out constant, unadorned signals about your internal condition to your audience. If you're nervous or don't believe what you're saying, the audience will pick up on it quickly. Focus on your nonverbal communication: stand tall, take deep breaths, smile, and look people in the eyes without flinching. Avoid slanting your body towards each leg or making awkward gestures. When delivering introductions, many people like to speak from behind a podium. While platforms are useful for collecting notes, they create a barrier between you and the audience. They may also serve as "support," providing you with a place to hide from the crowds of onlookers. Instead of staying behind a platform, go around and make eye contact with the audience. This growth and vitality will be reflected in your voice, which will become more vibrant and joyful.

When it comes to first impressions, nonverbal communication has the power to help us succeed or fail. We may succeed if we recognize and set out to exploit our nonverbal communication fully, or we can fail if we allow our nonverbal communication to take control of us. When you're practicing your speech, don't forget to work on your nonverbal communication as well. You'll feel pleasant, relaxed, and certain that you have what it takes to promote your show when it arrives! In terms of nonverbal communication in introductions, there are now many opposing viewpoints. There's the non-verbal communication of the moderator (you), and there's the non-verbal communication of your audience. The advice I'll provide you later in this post will be beneficial to either you or your audience. You'll discover how to be a fantastic moderator, but you'll also be able to look across and see how your audience reacts to your show. Knowing how to read a crowd is a wonderful skill and will come in handy in the future. You don't have to become one of those administrators who think they're doing a good job in front of the public when they're draining them!

Ask Questions in Public Speaking

Most audience questions are an inevitable part of most introductions, and presenters should be prepared for them. Questions indicate that the audience is interested and wants to learn more. Furthermore, whether or not someone has to confront you on a topic suggests that they were paying attention! Many inexperienced speakers ask questions at the end of their introductions. This is understandable, yet it is also a blunder. One of the most important aspects of your performance is your choice. It's your final opportunity to actually make an impression on your audience. You should keep a close eye on it and not relinquish control.

When you finish your experience on stage in a Q&A (Q&A) design, the final impact that you get is often reduced from what it would have been in some manner. This is especially true if you get inquiries that are off-topic or off-topic. Individuals in the audience begin fidgeting, checking their email, or, in any case, leaving. So, what are your options? Not answering questions is always a risk, but it's seldom a good one. Denying the audience, the opportunity to voice concerns with you will upset some and may jeopardize your credibility. Fortunately, there is a simple and effective arrangement: take questions just before your closing remarks.

Chapter 10. Characteristics of a Good Public Speaker

Public speaking is something that you will have to deal with for the rest of your life. You will have to give presentations of some sort for your whole educational life and even for some of the sports and other activities that you might be in. When you enter the workforce, you might have to do some public speaking to get a job, talk to the client, or even announce news on television. Many different types of public speaking are out there and there are many different situations where you might have to give a speech. Despite all of this, many people find that it is difficult to give a public speech. They might be worried that they will look bad while they are doing it, that they will forget their lines, or they just do not like to talk in front of other people. Even if you have these fears, it is important to learn how to get over them so that you are able to perform in your role. This can help you to see if you have some of these characteristics already; if not, you will be able to develop these characteristics in order to make speech giving easier. Some of the characteristics that are present in a good public speaker include:

- **Solid content**—even if you do not have a natural charisma about you like some speakers do, you will be able to get the audience on your side simply by having solid and valuable content to the audience. You need to make sure that all of the content you present will add value to the lives of the audience in some way. If you have a lot of fluff, just throw that out because it will make the audience bored and they will not take you seriously.

- **Humor**—people will always remember a speaker who was able to make them laugh. The earlier that you are able to get the audience smiling and laughing with you the more memorable your speech is going to be. This is because it will help make the audience around you more receptive to the ideas you are getting across. Having humor in your speech does not mean that you must be a comedian, just add in a few jokes and some irony and you are sure to get the audience on your side.

- **Organization**—before going out for a speech, you must make sure that you are completely organized. Have all of the facts checked, the information in order, and everything in its place. No excuse allows you to ramble on through the presentation. This is just going to make the audience get lost or make you lose your credibility. If you are organized, you leave your audience with a message that they can understand and which is easy to remember.

- **Approachable**—the best speakers are the ones who seem like they are approachable. These are the ones who will meet and greet people before and after the speech and who will leave room for questions at some point. These speakers do not seem like they are in a rush to leave right away but instead would rather spend their time with the audience.

- **Authentic**—people want to know who you are; they are smart enough to know when you are trying to pull one over on them and they will become less receptive if they feel like you are doing this. They want to hear someone who is going to be honest to them. If you are a shy person, it is fine to show this out a little in the speech because it lets people know that you feel that your message is important enough to share even though this is your fear.

- **Natural**—when you are up in front of an audience, you should try to act natural and calm. This will help the audience to feel like there is a connection and they will be able to listen more closely this way. It can often spell disaster if you are sitting there acting off or being too nervous. Try to act like the audience is some of your close friends and you are sharing something with them rather than worrying about a large crowd.

- **Passion**—a good speaker is someone passionate about what they are saying. They know that their information is valuable and useful and they want to get it out to the audience. When you are excited about the message, the audience will catch on to that excitement and be excited soon as well.

Chapter 11. Getting Audiences' Attention

"Self-assurance is alluring. It is strong and never fades, and that is far more intriguing than beauty.

I'm not sure whether you have ever encountered this, but in my case, I've had the good fortune to overhear some very remarkable communication interactions. The way I was mesmerized by the source of the message established the tone for them for me. These speakers always had a certain something. They exuded charm and an air that made you want to pay close attention to everything they said. It was not just what was said but also how it was conveyed—specifically, how the initial signals got to us—was important.

Why are certain individuals so captivating to us? If you think about it, it doesn't have anything to do with money or physical attractiveness. That is momentary. Even the most attractive person in the world will eventually have to speak, and if what comes out of it is a load of jumbled drivel, it will immediately turn us off.

People who are captivating are so by virtue of being there. They exude a certain gravitas and firmness in their demeanor and in the manner in which they convey what has to be said. They are skilled at making a point and doing so effectively. They put a lot of effort into what they do. Most importantly, they

They are certain of what they stand for. Ever hear the saying "confidence is sexy"? This is a maxim that alluring individuals are aware of and employ.

Another crucial aspect is that compelling presenters convey their words with genuine emotion. They express themselves honestly. It is sometimes believed that the first conversation you have with someone, and more specifically, the first few minutes of this first interaction, will reveal all you need to know about them. You actuallyhave a short amount of time to grab your audience's attention and convince them to stay focused.

If you fail to do this, you will lose their attention and must work hard to get it back.

The most effective speeches play to the audience's preferences. You will engage the audience when you learn to communicate your heart and emotions within the bounds of reason (I don't expect you to start crying in front of them until the topic of conversation calls for it). There is a great difference between being honest in your expression and spilling your guts. It just requires being honest with what you say and letting the listener identify with it.

You can be real with them, so you'll have a sense of intimacy. When you demonstrate to them how vital it is to you, they will begin to realize that whatever you are talking about is essential to them as well. Presenters who speak from the heart understand how important it is to connect with their audience as soon as they step up to the podium. Make your presentation more intriguing and approachable for your audience by using interesting tales or anything else.

You are not compelled to tell the audience a personal story. People frequently think that their lives are not important enough to I justify telling their story.

But a story is always present. There is always something intriguing to write about, and any event in the world may be used to develop a story. The protagonist of your narrative can be someone you know. He or she can be someone you work with, a close buddy, or a distant acquaintance. It's possible that the person who is the focus of your story has no relation to you at all, yet their story serves as a fantastic example of the point you are trying to make.

You might be wonder, "What can I do to become more interesting?" if you are anything like me—I was as uncomfortable as they come.

This is a practice in developing self-love and self-assurance. When you learn to accomplish this, you will not only improve your communication skills but also have more confidence in what you have to say. It truly is a bad demonstration of how much we believe in ourselves when we are not sure of what we are saying to others. How can we expect others to believe in us if we do not?

Of course, a lot of this might change in the future. We acknowledge that there will always be some element of spontaneity in conversations, especially when we must think quickly.

However, regardless of how spontaneous our later actions may be, the goal of this practice is to increase our confidence in ourselves.

Conversation could be necessary. By doing this, we actually acknowledge that we can handle any topic, no matter how challenging.

Start this activity by allocating a regular hour each day for yourself. Try to adhere to this time slot.

Practice in front of a large mirror that can clearly display your face, upper torso, and hands.

Maintain a prepared topic in your head. Any topic is OK, although I would suggest starting with a general subject. Consider acting as though you are telling a friend about how your day has been going.

Keep your forward-facing gaze focused directly in front of you. Start talking.

Always start your speeches with a salutation, period. This can be anything, such as a straightforward "good morning," "good evening," or "hello."

Explain what you mean gently while keeping your head straight forward. Pronounce each word clearly, carefully, and distinctly.

Try to keep track of what you are saying in your thoughts while you talk. Make sure you are aware of every word you say and don't allow the discussion to control you.

What this experiment shows may surprise you. We frequently speak too quickly and fail to notice the words that are coming out of our mouths. This entails that we keep talking incoherently until we realize that we have forgotten the entirety of what we were attempting to communicate. This obviously has a detrimental impact on boosting confidence.

Start using other body parts, including your hands and eyes, as you get more at ease conversing with yourself in front of the mirror. Show how enthusiastic you are about something by using your hands. Pay attention to the eyes. If the subject is intriguing, grin while you talk.

Wait at least two weeks before actually moving on to a family member or close friend. The next phase of your workout to boost your confidence is this.

With the friend or family member, go through each step again and again until you feel at ease. Although it could take some more time, keep in mind that you are now making the shift from being insecure in front of people.

The stage finally arrives when you start speaking in front of other people. Don't blurt out anything hastily. Avoid talking about topics that have no bearing on how you are feeling right now.

Make yourself more noticeable by sharing an intriguing fact or gripping tale. Therefore, you become more relatable.

Interact and converse. If you're talking about deadlines, for instance, you may mention some of the challenges employees might have in fulfilling deadlines at their place of employment. If people can relate to proposals and ideas in the presentation, they are more likely to pay attention to them.

Use conversational language when delivering your message.

Be receptive to the opinions of others around you.

You'll soon be able to see that they are becoming more and more engrossed in what you have to say. When that time comes, you'll be confident that you're equipped to take on the world and enthrall everyone with your words. You could wind up surprising yourself with your level of influence!

We are always more drawn to fascinating people. We usually feel as though we can connect with these folks on a personal level because they always know how to make a conversation real and interesting.

Chapter 12. Manage Conversation with Everyone

The most powerful people work toward genuine buy-in and accountability rather than consistent approaches that only provide temporary influence. To effectively resolve conflict so that all parties are satisfied with the outcome, a person must concurrently hold all opposing ideas, opinions, and viewpoints as a top priority while being viable. A person's ability to accept the rival's logical and full-feeling perspectives and perceive how the argument seems to the next individual and react really and attitudinally is crucial to effective critical thinking and compromise. If a person can't see things from the perspective of others, their understanding of the situation is limited and insufficient. This was the conclusion of the speaker. The high-impact speakers follow the pattern of four steps. Step 1: Listen through your susceptible sides, and Stage 2: Strive for remarkable achievements. Step 3: Once you've completed the necessary tasks, go on to the next step. Step 4: Involve others within their there is covered here.

Consider being on one corner of a retail mall, say the east corner, near a cafe, to see why this development is crucial. Then imagine that you and a friend are at the further end of the shopping mall, near a toy store. Also, imagine that you're letting that person know where you are. Now picture stating to yourself, "To get where I now, start in the top east corner beside a restaurant." That doesn't seem promising, does it? Because that is where you are, and not important where the other person is. That is, however, the method through which we typically seek to convince people based on our circumstances, presumptions, and experiences. We provide our point of view based on our perspective. Although there is a communication chasm between them and us, we act as though they are now on our part of the chasm. There are a hundred ways to start a conversation with anyone.

Different Ways to Start a Conversation

There are common topics that help anyone to start a healthy conversation with anyone.

Weather Discussion

Weather discussion is very common between two or more two people. If you went to someplace where you are not familiar with anyone, you want to start a conversation. You need a common topic that has no negative comments. To start with a weather discussion is a fabulous idea. You can discuss the current situation. You don't need anything to learn, or you don't need anything to ask from anyone else. You have to observe your surroundings and begin your conversation by discussing weather conditions. Climate change is the only exception to the no-negatives rule. If you're in the middle of a heatwave, a cold spell, or a torrential downpour, bringing up the unusual weather is a good way to start a conversation - it's a frequent thing that you and the listener are experiencing. If it's a really lovely day, that's also a good way to get things started.

Talk with positivity

To make a positive comment on any event is a good idea to start a healthy conversation. If you visited an event and another person also came from that event, you can give them positive feedback regarding the previous event.

Beginning with a positive comment like "This dive is delectable!" "For this occasion, there was a decent crowd!" "Have you listened to the featured discussion? It was fantastic, in my opinion." In almost every situation, there is something nice to say, so locate it and tell it. Try not to say anything bad since it might backfire if the audience turns out to be the published expert's cousin. "I thought the function was tiring," for example, could backfire if the audience turns out to be the published expert's cousin.

Ask for Information

To start a conversation, you can ask about any information. If you come to an event after some time, then you can ask about the event. You can ask that what happened before this? If you come someplace with your friends and people already eating food, so before buying you can ask about the quality of food or environment of sitting. You can ask, "Excuse me; however, do you know when the following meeting starts?" Even when you hear the appropriate response, mentioning data might be a magnificent procedure to get somebody to address you since everybody appreciates feeling helpful.

Offer Assistance

When you are not able to control yourself, all you want is to talk with another person. You can offer any guidance or assistance. You can show the right direction; you can ask to offer any assistance. You can give positive feedback to their dressing sense or any other thing. You won't often find yourself in a situation where you can assist someone passing away to communicate with you, but if you do, don't miss out on the chance to aid. "Would you want me to help you in transporting that massive box?" "Do you want to take a seat? There's one here that's free." "Do you want to see a program? As a result, I have an extra an." Since you've aided, the listeners will be inclined to like and trust you. Be cautious not to be intrusive or excessive. "I couldn't help but notice that your Visa had been denied - would you want to use mine?" will cause more havoc than anything else.

Ask for Assistance

You can share your services to start a conversation. You can tell them about what you would have. You can offer assistance in multiple ways to start a healthy conversation. "Would you be able to go there a first-class for me?" "My ring fell to the floor, and I believe it landed beneath your table. Would you want to look into it?" Requests for assistance are another way to make someone feel helpful. Make sure that everything you ask for is something that the audience can deliver without much difficulty.

Ask for Opinion

If you want to start a conversation with others and don't have any specific topic, you can ask for their opinion. You can ask them about work previous or continued work, you can ask them about your home, you can ask them about your vehicle or anything. You can ask, "How did you feel about the debate?" "Did this studio provide you with a lot of value?" "I notice you're sipping on a fantastic cocktail. Would you recommend it?"

Discuss Shared Experience

The listener put his complete effort into discussing the shared experience because both are connected with this experience. Is the audience from the same town or region as you? Did you follow a similar secondary school timetable daily? Have you both been employed for the same organization by the same boss?

Discuss Mutual Acquaintance

To start a healthy conversation, you may start with a discussion of mutual acquaintances. "Did you ever work with Roger before? I've participated in a few things with him." By naming someone you both know, you're signaling to the audience that you're important to their large network of friends. However, be certain that their connection with your mutual colleague is in good standing - you wouldn't want to suggest you're best friends with someone merely to develop familiarity with them when the audience is engaged in a serious dispute.

Appreciate the Listener

This is useful when deciding what to speak to a Celebrity, a well-known VC, or someone in your sector or company. "I adore your job" or, "I think your previous blog piece was incredibly clever" will never offend someone.

Three conditions: don't grovel, and don't judge the listeners, as in "I felt your current picture was considerably better than last year's." Also, if you're serious about not making a joke about it, you may want to acknowledge it. To appreciate the listener is a useful technique for the beginning of the discussion.

Effective Discussion

Managers that invest time and effort in communicating clear lines of communication can rapidly build confidence among employees, resulting in increased efficiency, yield, and overall certainty. Meanwhile, representatives who can effectively communicate with partners, executives, and customers are continually valuable resources for an organization. It is a skill that may commonly distinguish people from their competitors when competing for employment. When a piece of information is transmitted and received exactly, it becomes powerful communication. Just because you believe you're effectively communicating concepts and facts in your organization doesn't guarantee it's practical. Great communication may foster collaboration and increase the likelihood of task collaboration. It applies to almost every sector. The importance of work environment communication in smoothing out internal correspondence cannot be overstated. Maintaining effective communication ensures that management and the people who work for them are on the same page. This means that reps are confident in their current job, and managers may be certain that their coworkers have correctly accepted it.

However, keep in mind that communication in the workplace and commercial correspondence are two different things. Both are necessary for a company's future success. In the workplace, communication isn't just about how effectively you collaborate with others. It has to do with making connections, avoiding errors, and, most importantly, performing as efficiently as possible. As a pioneer, among the most crucial things you can do, is empower outstanding communication proclivities across the workplace. Within a company, the importance of good communication is enormous. The following are the five major reasons why you should pay attention:

Everyone Has Right to Speak

Employee satisfaction mostly depends on their having free speech and being heard, whether it's about a notion they've had or a criticism they need to express. Grounded communication channels should ensure that everyone can communicate freely with their friends, acquaintances, and employers regardless of their status.

Revolution

Workers who are free to express themselves without fear of ridicule or retaliation are inextricably compelled to provide ideas that may be useful. Advancement is heavily reliant on it, and an organization that energizes communication is unquestionably certain to be inventive.

Team Boosting

It's all about how those coworkers communicate and work together to form engaging groupings.

Effective Management

Supervisors who are excellent communicators are better equipped to cope with their teams. When you are a good communicator, assigning tasks, resolving conflicts, inspiring others, and building relationships (all key responsibilities of any administrator) become a lot easier. Solid communication isn't only the ability to address people; it's also the ability to get them to contact one other through solid openness channels.

Progress

Both inside and remotely, correspondence may be seen. By being registered inside and having reliable lines of communication, you can ensure that the message you're sending from afar is consistent. Any development project relies on good communication and all partners, internal and external, operating at the same frequency.

How to Improve Communication Skills of Individual or Organization?

Whether you're a startup or a little business, having excellent communication from beginning to end is critical. Understanding a shared meaning is an important part of establishing wonderful communication. This refers to how each person involved interprets the real facts, using words that imply the same thing to everyone, especially regarding industry-specific wording. Even managers have difficulty transferring information.

We recognize the value of effective communication. We've highlighted a few important areas where associations might enhance and upgrade communication amongst their groups below.

Clarification or Clarity in Goals

Please don't take it for granted that the other person understands what you're saying. Also, if you need clarification on anything, don't be afraid to speak out. Posing questions may help you better understand unique situations, and you should always allow your reps to inquire if they are unsure. This will help strengthen relationships with employees, but it will also help reduce errors. A simple query to double-check may sometimes prevent blunders from happening.

Make sure your communication is consistent and accessible to your target audience. To do so, you must speak clearly and considerately, expressing yourself clearly without causing confusion or offense.

Explain Expectations Via Meetings

Administrators must communicate clear, achievable goals to both groups and individuals, demonstrating exactly what is required on each given project and ensuring that all employees are aware of the venture's, division's, and organization's overall goals. It seems basic, yet it is often not well-rehearsed. The capacity to pay attention to people seems to be the most important correspondence skill you may have. If you notice that you tend to speak over people, make an effort to be more tolerant. When they're done, you'll have the opportunity to arrive at your important conclusion, particularly if you're the boss.

When employees feel valued and appreciated, they feel more valued and appreciated, which leads to a more common culture. It also gives you the chance to receive questions or concerns about an errand from a worker's perspective. This may help to increase employee commitment.

Convey Medium Carefully

Once you've created your message, you'll want to make sure it's delivered in the best possible way.

Listen to Others Point of View

Another desirable communication skill to have been receptivity. It allows you to join a conversation without preconceptions or judgments, allowing the person speaking the confidence to explain innovative ideas that might benefit the company.

If you're in a hurry to shut things down, reps will be less likely to share their opinions with you. Your conversations will be less authentic and beneficial in this regard. By having an open mind, you'll be prepared to engage in a conversation with someone whose opinion you may not agree with, and you could surprise yourself before the conversation is through. Communication is a two-way street, and no organization or person will last longer if they do not listen to and stimulate dialogue with the other side. Listening shows respect and allows you to learn about any unusual challenges your company may have.

Chapter 13. Ways to Connect with a Large Audience

Audience wants to laugh

Using comedy to connect with an audience is one of the greatest and easiest methods to do it. Remember that your audience does not want to be serious and wants to laugh now and then. You can bring on a lot of energy by making jokes and rewarding your audience with funny one-liners. Your audience will respond to your speech more enthusiastically and give you the confidence to keep going the same way.

Go slow

Apart from the number of words, you should also focus on the tempo and ensure that you go slowly so that every member of your audience gets the chance to hear what you are saying. Because it will take some time for your words to reach everyone in the room, you should slow down a little and ask your audience whether they can hear what you're saying.

Energy levels

Make sure you have a filling meal before addressing a large audience, as you have to keep your energy levels up. A large audience will give off and require high levels of energy to keep the show going. You have to make sure that you become louder as you go and come across as a strong speaker. Keep your energy levels high throughout the speech and crank it up a few notches after every subsequent pause. You should be able to feed off your audience's energy so that you can keep them motivated and interested in listening to what you have to say.

Simplicity is key

When you address a large crowd, you have to bear in mind that there will be people from all walks of life. Some might not be able to grasp high concepts and end up misinterpreting your jokes. You should, therefore, keep it simple so that everybody understands what you are saying and can respond to your speech positively.

Interactive

When addressing a large audience, you must make the session as interactive as possible. It is the only way in which you can keep everybody interested and keep going. Your speech should make you sound enthusiastic and full of energy and ask your audience to participate as much as they can. You should feed off their questions and answers and keep addressing them throughout the speech. If you make it all about yourself then you will end up driving across the wrong message and make it sound like you are boasting about yourself.

Be assertive

You should be as assertive as possible when it comes to speaking to a large audience. Many people make the error of asking too many questions in an effort to gain the audience's favor. This will make you appear nervous and make your audience think that you are not well prepared. So be assertive in whatever you say and avoid asking our audience if they agree with you. You have to make them agree with you without pushing it. So instead of asking, "What do you think?" you should tell them "This is what I want you to think."

Don't be overwhelmed

It is obvious that the higher the number of people in the audience, the more the difference there will be in opinions. It's very important not to get caught up in it and to keep your cool while speaking with them. It would be best if you got your audience to come to you rather than you going to them. You can easily do this by being assertive and telling your audience that you are decided on your stand, and they will have to accept it.

Get into character

Think of getting into your character when addressing your audience. Have an idea of what you wish to appear like to your audience and then get into full character mode for them. That way, you will know the parameters to stick with and can modify your approach to suit the needs of your audience. You can look up a few videos to help you out. Remember to enjoy yourself and not be too stringent trying to play a character on stage.

Clarify from time to time

If your audience ever had any questions or concerns, ask them straight away and address them. This will give you the confidence to continue ahead without worrying about whether or not your audience comprehended what you were saying. Once everything is clear you can proceed to the next concept with confidence.

Conclusion

Perhaps the actual and most important part of communication is the magic that happens in the space between one person's idea and another person's interpretation. Some people might be assertive, and some people might be passive; some might not know how to use their voice, while others have a tendency to dominate conversations. The following is a list of tips for effectively communicating with others.

1. **Be aware of your feelings:** Defining what makes you angry or upset isn't always easy, but it can often provide insight into how you might interact with someone else.

2. **Don't over-complicate things:** Most people make assumptions and conclusions based on a few initial thoughts. When interacting with someone else, it's important to remember that there is no need to explain or justify every feeling. Let the other person decide for himself how he feels about your first impression.

3. **Communicate with empathy:** Empathy is understanding the feelings of another person and communicating how you feel without trying to get them to change their course of action. If the other person isn't receptive to this idea, it will be difficult for him or her to understand your position. However, if they use this technique, it will enable you both to better communicate what needs to be done.

4. **Don't be overly aggressive:** This tactic will cause an inordinate amount of stress for the other person. It is important to be effective, but it is also important to not take away from the other person's ability to express ideas. Too much aggression can cause a lot of unnecessary stress and conflict.

5. **Don't be too passive:** This tactic will cause an inordinate amount of stress for the other person. When not being assertive, it is often best to avoid

trying to have an impact on things that aren't under your control. Avoid getting caught up in emotional reactions to situations or occurrences that have nothing to do with you.

6. **Use silence to your advantage:** Silence can be a very effective tool in communicating with others. When others are talking, it is important to avoid interrupting them. This will allow the other person to clarify his or her perspective and assist you in finding a solution that is acceptable to all sides.

7. **Communication comes in many shapes and sizes:** For some people, effective communication is much easier than it is for others. The first step is understanding what type of person you are dealing with before trying to communicate ideas with them. If you struggle to assert yourself, it might be best to avoid certain types of people. If you tend to dominate conversations, it might be best to avoid situations that require you to have a lot of influence or control.

8. **Offer options:** A conversation should be a two-way process in which both people present ideas and receive information. Asking questions is a crucial aspect of having a fruitful discussion, and paying attention to the

other person will ensure that they grasp your point. Sometimes simply asking for clarification is enough, but when there are multiple options or explanations for what has happened, it might be helpful if both parties gave their opinions so that each individual can better understand what has happened.

Printed in Great Britain
by Amazon